Original title: 101 STRANGE BUT TRUE NBA FACTS

101

STRANGE BUT TRUE

NBA FACTS

INCREDIBLE AND
SURPRISING EVENTS.

1

Kobe Bryant is one of the best in history and was selected at the 13th position in the 1996 Draft.

As if it wasn't incredible enough, 13 teams overlooked Kobe Bryant.

The team that selected him was not the Lakers (with whom he would play for 16 years), but the Charlotte Hornets.

However, in a trade, the Hornets exchanged the freshly graduated high school guard for Vlade Divac.

2

**Boston Celtics and New York Knicks are two of the most
iconic and historic teams in the NBA.**

The Celtics were founded in 1946 and the Knicks in the same year,
being two of the original eight teams in the NBA.

Since then, both teams have won numerous championships
and have featured some of the most famous and
talented players in NBA history.

The Celtics have won a total of 17 championships, tying them with
the Los Angeles Lakers as the team with the most NBA titles.

Among their most notable players are Bill Russell, Larry Bird,
Paul Pierce, and Kevin Garnett, among others.

The Celtics have maintained a great rivalry with the Lakers over
the years, competing in several finals between the two teams.

For their part, the Knicks have won two championships,
the first in 1970 and the second in 1973.

Throughout their history, they have featured legendary players
such as Walt Frazier, Willis Reed, Patrick Ewing,
and Carmelo Anthony, among others.

The Knicks have also maintained great rivalries with teams
like the Chicago Bulls and the Miami Heat.

Both teams have had ups and downs in their performance in
recent decades, but they remain two of the most recognized
and beloved franchises by NBA fans.

3

Muggsy Bogues is the shortest player in NBA history at a height of 1.60 meters, while Manute Bol is one of the tallest players at a height of 2.31 meters.

They played together on the Washington Bullets during the 1987-1988 season, which was the only season they shared as teammates.

In addition to his height, Manute Bol was known for his shot-blocking ability and uncommon three-point shooting for a player of his size.

Muggsy Bogues, on the other hand, excelled in his speed and ball-handling skills despite his short stature.

4

Despite his short stature, Muggsy Bogues had a successful career in the NBA.

After being drafted in the first round of the 1987 NBA Draft by the Washington Bullets, Bogues played for various teams, including the Charlotte Hornets and Toronto Raptors.

His strong point was his ability to assist his teammates, as he led the league in assists per game during the 1989-1990 season.

Additionally, Bogues is known for his appearance in the movie "Space Jam" alongside Michael Jordan and other NBA players.

5

The NBA logo was created in 1969 by Alan Siegel, who used Lakers player Jerry West as a model.

West was known for his on-court abilities and his nickname "Mr. Clutch," due to his ability to score in decisive moments.

Despite reaching the NBA Finals several times, he did not win a championship until his eighth season in the league in 1972.

Siegel created the logo based on a photograph of West dribbling with his right hand, but he inverted it so the player was dribbling with his left hand for better balance and symmetry in the design.

The logo has become one of the most iconic in sports history, and has been used by the NBA ever since.

6

Kareem Abdul-Jabbar and Shaquille O'Neal are two of the most dominant players in the center position in NBA history.

Abdul-Jabbar played for 20 seasons in the league, while O'Neal played for 19.

Both players won multiple championships, with Abdul-Jabbar having six rings and O'Neal having four.

Despite being tall and dominant players, three-point shooting was not one of their specialties.

Abdul-Jabbar attempted only one three-pointer in his entire career and missed it, while O'Neal had a career mark of 1 for 22 in three-pointers.

Nevertheless, both players are considered some of the best in NBA history due to their dominance in other aspects of the game, such as rebounding, blocking, and scoring.

7

The largest margin of victory in an NBA game.

The game between the Memphis Grizzlies and the Oklahoma City Thunder in which the Grizzlies won by 73 points (152-79) was actually the most lopsided in NBA history.

This record surpassed the previous one from December 17, 1991, when the Cleveland Cavaliers defeated the Miami Heat by 68 points (148-80).

In that game, the Cavs had an excellent performance from Hot Rod Williams, who scored 27 points, grabbed 8 rebounds, and dished out 4 assists in just 25 minutes of play.

8

A small number of NBA teams have never experienced the excitement of selecting first overall during the Draft since the system was established in 1966.

They are the following: Denver Nuggets, Indiana Pacers, Memphis Grizzlies, Miami Heat, Oklahoma City Thunder, and Utah Jazz.

Although some of them have managed to select great players and have success in the league, such as the Miami Heat who won three championships in 2006, 2012, and 2013.

Other teams, like the Utah Jazz, have had a successful history with iconic players like Karl Malone and John Stockton, but have never been able to win an NBA championship.

9

In the 1995 Finals, the world got to see two of the greats compete:

Hakeem Olajuwon, one of the most complete centers in NBA history, and Shaquille O'Neal, who would become one of the most dominant forces in the league.

Olajuwon's Rockets won the championship, leaving Shaq with a bitter taste in his mouth and prompting him to send a note to Hakeem after the Finals ended.

In the note, he invited him to play one-on-one so that he wouldn't have his team behind him supporting him.

The news went viral, and the event was going to be televised as a pay-per-view, but it was eventually canceled and only remained in the record of curious moments in the NBA.

10

Derrick Rose is an American professional basketball player who currently plays as a point guard for the NBA's New York Knicks.

Rose was selected as the first overall pick in the 2008 NBA Draft by the Chicago Bulls and quickly became one of the standout players in the league.

In the 2010-2011 season, Rose led the Bulls to a record of 62 wins and 20 losses and became the youngest player to win the NBA Most Valuable Player (MVP) Award at the age of 22.

In that season, he averaged 25 points, 7.7 assists, and 4.1 rebounds per game.

Unfortunately, Rose's career has been plagued by injuries, which has affected his ability to play consistently over the years.

Despite this, he has managed to remain relevant in the league and has been a key player on several teams, including the New York Knicks.

11

Stephen Curry, also known as "Steph," is a professional basketball player for the NBA's Golden State Warriors.

He was born on March 14, 1988, in Akron, Ohio, USA.

He is considered one of the best three-point shooters in NBA history and has broken numerous records in his career.

In the 2015-2016 season, Curry had an exceptional season, averaging 30.1 points, 5.4 rebounds, and 6.7 assists per game.

He led the Warriors to a regular season record of 73-9, surpassing the previous record set by the 1995-1996 Chicago Bulls, and led the team to the NBA Finals.

Curry was named the NBA Most Valuable Player (MVP) of the regular season for the second consecutive year and became the first player in history to be named MVP unanimously, receiving all the votes from the 121 journalists who participated in the voting.

In addition, Curry has been selected for the NBA All-Star Game multiple times, has been named to the All-NBA First Team multiple times, and has won several NBA championships with the Warriors.

He is considered one of the best players currently and has left his mark on the history of basketball.

12

Bill Russell.

He is considered one of the greatest basketball players of all time.

He played in the NBA for 13 seasons, all with the Boston Celtics, and during that time he won 11 championships, making him the most successful player in league history.

Russell also won five NBA Most Valuable Player Awards and was selected to the All-Star Game 12 times.

In addition to his on-court achievements, Russell was a leader and advocate for civil rights off the court.

He was an active supporter of racial equality and participated in marches and protests during the 1960s civil rights movement.

After retiring as a player, Russell also worked as a coach in the NBA and NCAA. In his honor, the NBA Finals Most Valuable Player Award trophy is named after him.

It is a recognition of his skill as a player and his impact on the league and society as a whole.

13

Larry O'Brien was one of the most influential commissioners in NBA history, and his legacy is still felt in the league today.

In addition to the merger with the ABA and the establishment of the salary cap, O'Brien also helped expand the league, adding six new teams during his tenure.

He also worked to improve the NBA's image, promoting greater racial diversity in the league and helping to resolve labor disputes.

O'Brien passed away in 1990, and the trophy named after him was introduced in 1984 to honor the NBA champion.

14

Gregg Popovich.

He is the NBA coach who has earned
the most money in his career to date.

Popovich, who has been the head coach of the
San Antonio Spurs since 1996, has won five NBA
championships with the team and has been
named NBA Coach of the Year three times.

In addition, he has coached the United States
men's basketball team in several international
events, including the 2020 Olympics.

As for NBA coach salaries, it is true that they
have increased significantly in recent years.

According to a 2021 ESPN report, the average
salary for NBA coaches is around $6 million
per year, with some coaches earning
much more than that.

In addition, the most successful and experienced
coaches tend to earn higher salaries.

15

Bob McAdoo and Moses Malone are the most "well-traveled" MVPs in history.

In contrast to MVPs who played for just one team, such as Tim Duncan, Bill Russell, Dirk Nowitzki, Larry Bird, or Magic Johnson, Bob McAdoo and Moses Malone played for seven different teams.

McAdoo initially played for the Buffalo Braves (now the Clippers) where he became MVP in 1975, and subsequently played for the Knicks, Celtics, Pistons, Nets, Lakers, and Philadelphia 76ers.

On the other hand, Moses Malone, after starting his career in the ABA, briefly played for the Buffalo Braves for only two games, then went on to play for the Houston Rockets where he was a two-time MVP, the Philadelphia 76ers where he also became MVP and won his only NBA championship, the Washington Bullets, Atlanta Hawks, Milwaukee Bucks, and San Antonio Spurs.

16

The longest winning streak in the history of the competition.

The Los Angeles Lakers set a record of 33 consecutive victories in the 1971-1972 season, winning every regular-season game from November 5, 1971, to January 9, 1972, when they finally lost to the Milwaukee Bucks.

The record of those Lakers is so impressive that neither Michael Jordan's 72-10 Chicago Bulls nor the Splash Brothers' 73-9 Golden State Warriors could surpass the epic record set by the 1972 Lakers, who ultimately became NBA champions.

17

Wilt Chamberlain.

Born in 1936 and died in 1999, he is considered one of the greatest basketball players of all time.

He was one of the most dominant players of his era, playing in the NBA from 1959 to 1973.

Chamberlain played for three different teams during his career: the Philadelphia Warriors, the San Francisco Warriors, and the Los Angeles Lakers.

He set several records that still stand today, including scoring 100 points in a single game, which he achieved in 1962 in a game between the Philadelphia Warriors and the New York Knicks.

He also holds the record for the highest scoring average in a single season with 50.4, achieved in the 1961-1962 season, as well as the record for most rebounds in a game with 55.

In addition to his dominance on the court, Chamberlain was also a civil rights advocate and fought for racial equality in the United States.

After retiring from basketball, Chamberlain dabbled in acting, music, and business and became a very popular figure in American popular culture.

18

The NBA Draft is an annual event where teams in the league select new players to join their teams.

Since the creation of the NBA in 1949, the Draft has been a major source of talent for the league and has produced many star players and future Hall of Famers.

However, the 2000 Draft has been considered one of the worst in NBA history.

In that Draft, teams selected players who did not have a great career in the NBA and did not have much impact in the league.

Some of the players selected in the 2000 Draft include Kenyon Martin, Stromile Swift, Darius Miles, Marcus Fizer, and Chris Mihm.

Although some of these players had decent careers in the NBA, none of them became a league star or an All-Star player.

Compared to other NBA Drafts, the 2000 Draft was considered a disappointment due to the lack of talent and impact that many of the selected players had in the league.

19

Stephen Curry is known as one of the greatest shooters in NBA history and has set several three-point records throughout his career.

In the 2015-2016 season, he set the record for most three-pointers in a regular season with 402, surpassing his own previous record of 286.

He is also the first player in NBA history to have at least 300 three-pointers in a season.

As for the career three-point record, Curry surpassed Ray Allen as the fastest player to reach 2,000 three-pointers in 2016, and has since continued to add to his record.

In April 2021, Curry scored his 2,973rd three-pointer, surpassing Reggie Miller as the second-highest three-point scorer in NBA history.

Currently, he has more than 3,000 three-pointers scored in his career.

20

Former NBA player Gerald Green and Latvian player Dāvis Bertāns have something in common.

Both players are missing a finger from one hand, specifically their ring finger.

Green lost his finger at the age of 11 when he was attempting a dunk on his home basketball hoop and his ring got caught on a nail, causing his finger to be completely severed and ultimately amputated.

Bertāns cut off the top half of his finger at the age of 13 while chopping wood with his brother and his glove got caught in a saw.

21

Sports Illustrated published a report stating that 60% of retired NBA players go broke within 5 years of retirement.

Some examples include Allen Iverson, Dennis Rodman, Latrell Sprewell, and Antoine Walker.

Most of them failed to properly manage their wealth and ended up spending their money until they declared bankruptcy.

The average age of NBA players retiring is around 30 years old, though recently it has been increasing.

For example, Nat Hickey retired at 45, Steve Nash at 40, and Kareem Abdul-Jabbar at 42.

22

The NBA championship ring is awarded to the players on the team that wins the league each year.

The player with the most NBA championship rings is currently Bill Russell, who turned 84 years old in 2022, with 11 rings.

The second player with the most rings is Sam Jones, 88 years old in 2022, with 10, and the third is John Havlicek, who passed away in 2019, with 8 rings.

All three players won their rings while playing for the Boston Celtics during the same seasons.

On the other hand, Michael Jordan has 6 rings and Magic Johnson has 5.

23

A basket in an NBA game is located 3.05 meters high.

The backboard that holds the rim measures 1.05 meters high and 1.80 meters wide and has a thickness of 3 cm.

Why this height? It turns out that the inventor of basketball, James Naismith, hung two peach baskets on a balcony of a gymnasium at this height in 1891, and it has remained in the official NBA regulations ever since.

In 1954, the NBA conducted tests to make the game more dynamic and tried to place the basket at 3.65 meters in a game between the Minneapolis Lakers and the Milwaukee Hawks.

What happened is that both teams scored fewer points than their usual average, and the idea remained as a footnote in NBA history.

24

The possession of the ball per player is 24 seconds, a rule established in 1954 when they sought to give more excitement and speed to the game to attract more fans.

In addition, the famous clock was included, which counts every second so that players get more nervous and pass the ball faster.

Now you have learned some of the curiosities of the historic NBA basketball league.

Every year, the best players face each other on the court in high-adrenaline games for fans.

Betting odds in NBA games are a way to add more interest and excitement to this game.

25

The NBA appeared in 1949 from the merger of the BAA (Basketball Association of America) and the NBL (National Basketball League).

In its first season, it had 17 teams mainly from the NBL. In turn, the BBA was born in 1946 after World War II, at the hands of the main owners of sports stadiums in the northeast of the United States.

Ice hockey and boxing were not bringing them enough profits, and they needed an extra activity that complemented the previous two.

Thus, this sport was born with 13 teams.

This is the date used when talking about the founding of the NBA.

After the merger between the BAA and NBL, franchises began to decline, and in the 1953/54 season, the NBA had the lowest number of teams in its history: 8.

All of them are still in the league today.

26

The first NBA game is considered to have been played on November 1, 1946, at Maple Leaf Gardens in Toronto, Canada.

The game was between the Toronto Huskies and the New York Knicks, with the Knicks winning 68-66.

The first basket in NBA history was scored by Ossie Schectman, a player for the Knicks.

At that time, the NBA was known as the Basketball Association of America (BAA) and consisted of 11 teams, five of which were located in Canadian cities.

The BAA championship was played in a single playoff series, where the winners of the Eastern and Western divisions faced off in the Finals.

In 1949, the BAA merged with the National Basketball League (NBL) to form the current National Basketball Association (NBA), which included 17 teams.

Since then, the NBA has grown in popularity and become one of the most important and lucrative sports leagues in the world.

27

The NBA (National Basketball Association) is a professional basketball league in the United States that was founded in 1946.

Since then, there have been many franchises that have entered and exited the league, and there are currently 30 teams in total.

Of these 30 teams, only three have been present in every season since 1946: the Boston Celtics, the New York Knicks, and the Golden State Warriors.

The Celtics were founded in 1946 and play in the city of Boston, while the Knicks and Warriors were founded in 1946 and 1947, respectively, and play in the cities of New York and San Francisco.

These three franchises are considered the most representative and historic in the league due to their longevity and success on the court.

The Celtics are especially notable for having won a record 17 NBA championships, while the Knicks and Warriors have also won multiple championships throughout their history.

Additionally, the Celtics and Knicks are the only two franchises still playing in the same city where they were founded, giving them a special connection to their local communities and a rich history in the city.

28

The world of professional basketball in the United States has historically been dominated by white players.

However, throughout the history of the NBA, there have been several important milestones in terms of racial diversity and inclusion in the league.

One of the most significant moments in this regard was the inclusion of the first "non-white" player in the NBA.

This was Wataru Misaka, a Japanese-American player who was signed by the New York Knicks in the 1947/48 season.

Despite being drafted by the NBA in 1947, Misaka played only three games with the Knicks before being cut from the team.

The first African American to play in the NBA was Harold Hunter, who played for the Washington Capitols in the 1950 season.

Despite being a talented player, Hunter failed to complete the season due to health issues and other factors.

From the inclusion of Hunter, a progressive process of inclusion of African American players in the NBA began.

In the following years, several outstanding black players, such as Bill Russell and Wilt Chamberlain, became stars in the league, and the NBA became an important showcase for the African American community.

Today, the NBA takes pride in its racial and cultural diversity, and has established initiatives to promote inclusion and equality in the league.

Additionally, the NBA has been a model for other professional sports leagues in the United States in terms of promoting diversity and inclusion in sports.

29

In 1967, the American Basketball Federation created the ABA (American Basketball Association) with the purpose of diminishing the importance of the NBA.

After a few years of intense back and forth, in 1976, a merger agreement was reached between both leagues.

The ABA disappeared, and 4 of its teams were integrated into the NBA.

In addition to these 4 teams, the ABA left three other legacies:

-The tricolored basketballs in the three-point contest of the All-Star Game.

-The slam dunk contest.

-The three-point line.

30

During the late 1970s and early 1980s, the NBA went through a difficult period.

The league was struggling with financial and audience issues, with low attendance rates at games and low TV ratings.

Many sports analysts believed that the league was in danger of disappearing.

However, in the 1979-1980 season, two young talented players made their appearance in the NBA: Larry Bird of the Boston Celtics and Magic Johnson of the Los Angeles Lakers.

These two players were not only incredibly talented, but they also had very different playing styles that captured the public's attention.

Bird, a white player from Indiana, was known for his ability to shoot from long distance and his court intelligence.

Johnson, an African-American player from Michigan, was a natural playmaker with a knack for passing and team play.

The rivalry between Bird and Johnson quickly intensified and became one of the greatest rivalries in sports history.

The two teams faced each other in three consecutive NBA finals in the 1980s, and the rivalry between Bird and Johnson helped propel the popularity of the NBA to unprecedented levels.

The rivalry between Bird and Johnson, along with other talented players of the era like Michael Jordan, helped revive the NBA and attract a wider audience.

The NBA became a cultural phenomenon and a model for other professional sports leagues around the world.

31

The NBA is made up of 30 teams or franchises that are divided into two conferences, the Eastern Conference and the Western Conference, and each conference is further divided into three divisions with five teams each.

In the Eastern Conference are the Atlantic, Central, and Southeast divisions, while in the Western Conference are the Northwest, Pacific, and Southwest divisions.

Each NBA team plays a total of 82 games in a regular season, facing teams from their own conference and also from the other conference.

The teams compete to secure a place in the playoffs, where the top eight teams from each conference face off in a series of eliminations to determine the NBA champion.

Of the 30 NBA teams, only one is located outside of the United States: the Toronto Raptors, who are based in Canada.

The Vancouver Grizzlies were also a Canadian franchise that played in the NBA until 2001, when they moved to Memphis and became the Memphis Grizzlies.

Additionally, some NBA teams have a long history and are considered part of the league's identity, such as the Boston Celtics, the Chicago Bulls, the Los Angeles Lakers, and the New York Knicks.

There are also more recent teams that have joined the league, such as the Charlotte Hornets, who returned to the NBA in 2004 after a brief hiatus in 2002, and the New Orleans Pelicans, who moved from Charlotte in 2002 and were previously known as the New Orleans Hornets.

32

During the Regular Season, each team plays 82 games, half at home and half away:

- 4 times against all the teams in their Division (4 x 4 = 16 games)

- 4 times against 3 teams from each of the other two Divisions (4 x 3 x 2 = 24 games)

- 3 times against the remaining 4 teams from the other Divisions (3 x 2 x 2 = 12 games)

- 2 times against each team from the other Conference (2 x 15 = 30 games).

33

The NBA is one of only two sports leagues in the United States that has a schedule in which each team plays at least once against every other team in the league during the regular season.

This type of schedule is known as a "round-robin" or "everyone plays everyone."

Prior to the 2004-2005 season, the NBA had a schedule structure in which each team in one conference only played against teams from the other conference twice a year, once at home and once away, meaning that teams did not face each other with the same frequency.

However, since the 2004-2005 season, the NBA changed its schedule structure and began scheduling games for each team against all other teams in the league.

This was done to increase competitiveness and equity among teams.

The NHL, on the other hand, has had a "everyone plays everyone" schedule since 1970.

Other major sports leagues in the United States, such as the NFL (American football) and MLB (baseball), have a schedule structure in which teams only play some of the other teams in the league during the regular season.

34

In the NBA, eight teams from each conference advance to the playoffs at the end of the regular season.

The selection of teams and determination of matchups are done as follows:

The three teams that win their division in each conference automatically advance to the playoffs and are seeded as the first three in their conference based on their win-loss record.

The remaining team with the best win-loss record among teams that did not win their division qualifies as the fourth seed in the conference.

The remaining four teams in each conference are seeded based on their win-loss record, regardless of whether they won their division or not.

These teams are seeded as the fifth, sixth, seventh, and eighth in the conference, respectively.

After the eight teams from each conference are established, matchups are made according to the following scheme:

the first seed plays the eighth seed, the second plays the seventh, the third plays the sixth, and the fourth plays the fifth.

Teams face off in a best-of-seven series, with the team with the better regular season record having home court advantage in the first two games and in a possible seventh game.

Teams that win a series advance to the next round, and so on until only one team per conference remains.

These two teams face off in the NBA Finals to determine the league champion.

35

**Phil Jackson is one of the most successful coaches
in the history of the NBA.**

Born in Montana, USA in 1945, Jackson is known for his relaxed
leadership style and his ability to bring his teams together.

Jackson began his career in the NBA as a player, being drafted in the
second round of the 1967 draft by the New York Knicks.

However, his playing career was short-lived due to injuries.

After retiring as a player, Jackson began coaching, starting in the
minor league Continental Basketball Association (CBA).

In 1987, Jackson joined the Chicago Bulls as an assistant coach,
and in 1989 he was named head coach of the team.

During his time with the Bulls, Jackson coached players like Michael
Jordan, Scottie Pippen, and Dennis Rodman, and led the team
to six NBA championships in the 90s.

Jackson's unique offensive system, known as the Triangle,
was a key factor in the Bulls' success.

After leaving the Bulls in 1998, Jackson took a brief break
from basketball before returning as head coach
of the Los Angeles Lakers in 1999.

With the Lakers, Jackson led the team to five NBA championships
in 11 seasons, including three consecutive titles in
2000, 2001, and 2002.

In total, Jackson has won 11 NBA championships in his coaching
career, making him the most successful coach in the league's history.

In 2014, Jackson retired from basketball after a brief stint as the
president of basketball operations for the New York Knicks.

36

Arnold "Red" Auerbach was an American basketball coach and executive born in 1917 and passed away in 2006.

He is considered one of the most influential coaches in NBA history.

During his coaching career, Auerbach led the Boston Celtics to nine NBA championships in the 1960s, including eight in a row from 1959 to 1966.

Auerbach was also known for his innovations in the game, including popularizing the zone defense and introducing screening plays.

He also emphasized the importance of teamwork and chemistry in the locker room and was famous for his shrewd draft picks.

After retiring as a coach, Auerbach became the president and general manager of the Celtics and helped build championship teams in the 1980s.

During his time with the Celtics organization, Auerbach selected players like Bill Russell, Larry Bird, and Kevin McHale, who became NBA legends.

In addition to his basketball achievements, Auerbach was a civil rights advocate and was one of the first coaches to give opportunities to African American players in the NBA.

He was inducted into the Basketball Hall of Fame in 1969 as a coach and in 1980 as a basketball contributor.

37

Attendance record: 2010 All-Star Game at Cowboys Stadium gathered 108,713 people where the Eastern Conference team won 141-139 against the West.

The combination of shooting guard Dwyane Wade, LeBron James, and small forward Chris Bosh allowed the Eastern Conference team to win 141-139 against the West in the 59th edition of the All-Star Game.

The absence of Kobe Bryant from the Los Angeles Lakers on the West team was noticeable, especially in the decisive moments of the last few minutes when the game was tied at 137-137.

38

Kareem Abdul-Jabbar is a retired American basketball player considered one of the greatest of all time.

He was born on April 16, 1947 in New York, and his birth name was Ferdinand Lewis Alcindor Jr. Abdul-Jabbar played in the NBA for 20 seasons, from 1969 to 1989, mainly with the Milwaukee Bucks and the Los Angeles Lakers.

During his career, he won six NBA championships, six NBA MVP awards, and was selected to the NBA All-Star Game 19 times.

In terms of his scoring record, Abdul-Jabbar scored 38,387 points in his career, surpassing the previous record held by Wilt Chamberlain.

Only six other players have surpassed the 30,000-point barrier in NBA history: Karl Malone, LeBron James, Kobe Bryant, Michael Jordan, Dirk Nowitzki, and current Brooklyn Nets player Kevin Durant.

In addition to his success on the court, Abdul-Jabbar is also known for his political and social activism, including his support for the civil rights movement and his opposition to the Vietnam War.

He has also been a prolific author, writing several books about his career and life off the court.

39

Michael Jordan.

He is considered one of the greatest basketball players
of all time, and his scoring average of 30.1 points
per game is the highest in NBA history.

During his career, he played in 15 seasons and averaged
30.1 points per game in the regular season and
33.4 points per game in the playoffs,
which is also an NBA record.

Jordan was the NBA's leading scorer 10 times and led the
league in scoring average in each of those seasons.

He is also the NBA's all-time leader in playoff points
per game, with an average of 33.4 points per game.

Jordan spent most of his career with the Chicago Bulls,
where he won six NBA championships and was named
the NBA Finals Most Valuable Player (MVP)
on all of those occasions.

He was also named the NBA regular season MVP five times.
In addition to his NBA achievements, Jordan also won two
Olympic gold medals with the United States men's
basketball team in 1984 and 1992.

Jordan is a member of the Basketball Hall of Fame and
his number 23 has been retired by the Chicago Bulls.

40

The Boston Celtics are the team with the most NBA championships in their history, with a total of 17 titles.

The team was founded in 1946 and won their first championship in the 1956-57 season.

During the 1960s, the team led by Bill Russell won a total of 11 championships in a 13-year period, which is considered one of the most impressive achievements in the history of sports.

On the other hand, the Los Angeles Lakers have 16 titles, including the five they won when they were still located in Minneapolis.

The Lakers have had iconic players in their history, such as Kobe Bryant, Magic Johnson, Shaquille O'Neal, and Kareem Abdul-Jabbar, among others.

Additionally, other teams with multiple NBA championships include the Chicago Bulls with 6 titles, the Golden State Warriors with 6, the San Antonio Spurs with 5, the Miami Heat with 3, the Detroit Pistons with 3, the Philadelphia 76ers with 3, and the Houston Rockets with 2.

41

Pat Riley.

He is one of the most successful coaches in NBA history.

During his coaching career, he led three different teams
to win the NBA championship:

the Los Angeles Lakers, Miami Heat, and New York Knicks.

During his time as the Lakers coach in the 1980s, Riley managed
to win four NBA championships in a span of eight years,
between 1982 and 1989.

During that time, he implemented a fast-paced and attractive style of
play that became his signature, and coached some of the NBA's
greatest legends, such as Magic Johnson and Kareem Abdul-Jabbar.

In 1995, Riley joined the New York Knicks, where he
continued to be a successful coach.

He led the team to the NBA Finals in 1999, although
they lost to the San Antonio Spurs.

Riley became known for his charismatic style and his ability to
motivate his players, which earned him the nickname "The Godfather."

In 2005, Riley returned to the NBA as president
and coach of the Miami Heat.

There, he built a team around superstar Dwyane Wade, and in 2006,
he managed to lead the Heat to their first NBA
championship in franchise history.

Riley continued to lead the team for several more years, and in 2012,
he led them to their second championship in four years.

42

Los Angeles Lakers (33 wins – 1971/72)

Jerry West and Wilt Chamberlain set a
record in the 1971-72 season that
still stands today.

That season, the Los Angeles Lakers
finished with a record of 69-13 and
won 33 consecutive games.

This winning streak propelled them to
finish the regular season as the best team
and ultimately win the championship by
defeating the New York Knicks 4-1.

Chamberlain was named the MVP of the
Finals with 19.4 points, 23.2 rebounds,
and 2.6 assists per game.

43

Golden State Warriors (28 wins – 2014/15 and 2015/16)

The three-time champion and five-time consecutive Finals contender Warriors are also on this list.

Between the 2014/15 and 2015/16 seasons, the Golden State Warriors won 28 consecutive games.

They won their last 4 games of the 2014/15 regular season, in which they became champions, and the first 24 games of the 2015/16 season, in which they set an NBA record by finishing the regular season with a 73-9 record.

44

Miami Heat (27 wins - 2012/13)

The Big Three of LeBron James, Dwyane Wade, and Chris Bosh took some time to get going, but once they did, they were unbeatable for a period.

In the 2012/13 season, just after winning their first championship, the Miami Heat won 27 consecutive games between February 3, 2013, and March 25, 2013.

That season, the Heat finished with their best record in franchise history (66-16) and won their second consecutive championship by defeating the San Antonio Spurs 4-3.

45

Houston Rockets (22 wins – 2007/08)

The duo of Tracy McGrady and Yao Ming never quite shined in the playoffs, but they had plenty of talent.

During the 2007/08 season, they had one of their best moments and earned a spot on this list by winning 22 consecutive games.

The streak, which started on January 30, 2008, was stopped by the Boston Celtics, who went on to win the championship.

The Rockets finished the regular season with a record of 55–27 and were eliminated in the first round of the playoffs, losing 4–2 to the Utah Jazz.

46

Milwaukee Bucks (20 wins – 1970/71)

Let's go back to the 20th century to talk about the Milwaukee Bucks of Oscar Robertson and Kareem Abdul-Jabbar.

In the 1970-71 season, the Bucks won 20 consecutive games, with an impressive performance by Kareem, who averaged 31.7 points, 16 rebounds, and 3.3 assists per game and was named the MVP under his former name Lew Alcindor.

In the Finals, they swept the Washington Bullets 4-0.

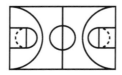

47

Washington Capitals (20 wins – 1947/48 and 1948/49)

Now we travel back to the early years of the NBA to the seasons between 1947/48 and 1948/49, when the Washington Capitols won 20 consecutive games.

Although they were a short-lived franchise, existing only from 1946 to 1951, they won 5 games in the 1947/48 season and 15 games in the 1948/49 season.

In the latter season, they made it to the Finals but lost to the Minneapolis Lakers 4-2.

48

Los Angeles Lakers (19 wins –1999/00)

In the modern NBA era of Shaquille O'Neal and Kobe Bryant's Lakers, who achieved the three-peat with Phil Jackson at the helm, it's worth highlighting that prior to the first of those three championships, the gold and purple shone on their own, winning 19 straight games that would lead them to a final record of 67-15, with Shaq averaging 29.7 points, 13.6 rebounds, 3.8 assists, and 3 blocks per night.

In the playoffs, they would beat the Philadelphia 76ers with a clear 4-1.

49

Boston Celtics (19 wins - 2007/08)

Another championship-winning team
that flexed their muscle during
the regular season.

The Celtics brought together Paul Pierce,
Kevin Garnett, and Ray Allen in the summer
of 2007 to win the ring and incidentally
make it into this classification by
winning 19 consecutive games.

With Doc Rivers at the helm, Boston would
finish the regular season with a record of
66-16 and in the Finals, they would
defeat the Lakers 4-2.

It was a very important moment for an
organization that hadn't won a
championship since 1986 with
Larry Bird at the helm.

50

San Antonio Spurs (19 wins – 2013/14)

The San Antonio Spurs, one of the great dynasties of the 21st century, had an excellent 2013/14 season in which they would become champions.

Let's remember that a year earlier, they lost the Finals to the Miami Heat after losing in a sixth game in which they were winning by three points with just a few seconds left, just until Ray Allen worked his magic.

A year later, they would win the championship ring and along the way achieve 19 straight wins.

Another statistic in favor of an enormous team led by Tim Duncan.

51

Atlanta Hawks (19 wins – 2014/15).

With Mike Budenholzer at the helm of operations, the Atlanta franchise thrilled with an excellent regular season that would end with a record of 60-22, stringing together 19 wins along the way.

Jeff Teague, Kyle Korver, Paul Millsap, Al Horford. In Georgia, they had fun with a team game that led them to the Conference finals, where they would fall to LeBron James' Cleveland Cavaliers 4-0.

52

Washington Bullets 44-38.

We have to go back to the late 1970s to find the leader of this ranking.

We go exactly to the 1977-78 season to remember the title won by the Washington Bullets that year.

Under the leadership of Elvin Hayes, who would play up to seven seasons in the capital, and with the no less important contribution of another Hall of Famer like Wes Unseld and shooting guard Bob Dandridge, the Bullets surprised everyone when they won the championship after finishing the regular season with a modest 44-38 record.

53

The St. Louis Hawks basketball team was founded in 1946 and participated in the National Basketball League (NBL) until 1949, when the league merged with the Basketball Association of America (BAA) to form the current NBA.

The Hawks became one of the most successful teams in the NBA in the 1950s and 1960s, led by stars like Bob Pettit and Cliff Hagan.

In 1958, the Hawks reached the NBA Finals and faced the Boston Celtics in an exciting six-game series, but ultimately lost the title.

Although the Hawks reached the Finals three more times in the 1950s and 1960s, they only managed to win the championship in 1958.

In 1968, the Hawks moved to Atlanta and have been known as the Atlanta Hawks since then.

Although the team has had ups and downs in its history, they have managed to reach the NBA Finals four more times since then, but without success in winning another title.

54

Houston Rockets.

The Houston Rockets of the 1994-95 season, just
after winning their first championship, had a
tumultuous regular season that only improved
with the arrival of veteran Clyde Drexler.

Despite this move, Rudy Tomjanovich's team finished
the season with an uneven 47-35 record, leaving
them sixth in the Western Conference with up to
nine teams having a better record than them.

These stats did not stop them.

On their way to their second consecutive
championship, and under the leadership of the
tremendous Hakeem Olajuwon, the team would win
in the first round against the Utah Jazz (60-22),
in the semifinals against the Phoenix Suns (59-23),
and in the conference finals against the
San Antonio Spurs (62-20).

In the grand final, they left no chance for the Orlando
Magic of Anfernee Hardaway and Shaquille O'Neal,
whom they swept 4-0 to become the first team in
history to eliminate four teams with over 50 wins
on their way to the championship.

55

Philadelphia Warriors.

The Philadelphia Warriors have the honor of being the team that inaugurates the list of championship winners, and interestingly enough, they did it by being beaten in the regular season by up to three teams that had a better record than them: the Washington Capitols (49-11), the Chicago Stags (39-22), and the St. Louis Bombers (38-23).

With Hall of Famer Joe Fulks as the main star, the Warriors would win the championship after defeating the Bombers, the Knicks, and Chicago, already in the finals, by 4-1.

As we say, Fulks was as decisive as his 22.2 points per game average in the playoffs indicates.

56

1948. Baltimore Bullets.

The Philadelphia Warriors were the victims in the final, as it was the Baltimore Bullets who ended up being the best team of the year after finishing the regular season with a 28-20 record.

It was a somewhat strange season, as there were up to six teams within two games of each other; furthermore, two other teams signed exactly the same number of wins and losses as those from the east of the United States (Chicago Stags and Washington Capitols).

Focusing on the playoffs, the Bullets had Connie Simmons as their main star, a player who came from Boston and averaged 17.1 points in the postseason before leaving for the New York Knicks in 1949.

57

1969. Boston Celtics.

With overwhelming dominance in the 60s, when they won nine rings in ten years, the 1968-69 campaign was one of those where everything was fixed in the playoffs.

Despite finishing the regular season with a 48-34 record that placed them behind four teams, including the Lakers (55-27), the greens made it clear in the postseason that they were mentally above all their rivals at that time.

Thus, they ended the hopes of the Philadelphia 76ers and New York Knicks before taking down the Lakers of Elgin Baylor, Jerry West and Wilt Chamberlain in the Finals 4-3.

58

The Golden State Warriors is an NBA franchise based in San Francisco, California.

The 1974-1975 season was one of the most memorable for the Warriors, as they won their second NBA championship in team history.

The squad was led by Rick Barry, who averaged 30.6 points per game during the regular season and was named Finals MVP.

Despite finishing the regular season with a modest record of 48-34, the Warriors ignited in the playoffs and eliminated the Seattle Supersonics, Chicago Bulls, and Houston Rockets on their way to the NBA Finals.

There, they faced the Washington Bullets, who had finished the regular season with a record of 60-22.

However, the Warriors surprised everyone by sweeping the Bullets in four games.

Rick Barry was named Finals MVP after averaging 29.5 points, 5.0 rebounds, and 4.3 assists per game during the series.

This championship remains one of the most remembered in Warriors history, and the team would not win another NBA championship until 2015.

59

1955 – Syracuse Nationals.

Based in the state of New York, this team competed in the NBA from 1949 to 1963, the year it was bought by an entrepreneur to move it to the Pennsylvania city where it currently resides.

In the 1954-55 campaign, they were champions.

With Hall of Fame Dolph Schayes as the star, the Nationals would finish the mentioned season with a record of 43-29.

It was not a great record, but it was enough to be the best team that year alongside the Fort Wayne Pistons.

In the postseason, they would beat them by 4-3 to achieve the only title of their Syracuse era.

Schayes was their best man in those playoffs, averaging 18.5 points and 12.3 rebounds.

60

In the 1976-1977 season, the Portland Trail Blazers won their first NBA championship by defeating the Philadelphia 76ers in six games in the Finals.

The Blazers were a relatively young and inexperienced team compared to their rivals, but they had a talented roster led by star shooting guard Bill Walton.

During the regular season, the Blazers finished with a record of 49-33, the fourth best record in the Western Conference.

However, in the playoffs, the Blazers became an unstoppable team, winning 12 of their 13 postseason games, including a 4-0 sweep over the Lakers in the Conference Finals.

In the NBA Finals, the Blazers faced a team of 76ers led by Julius Erving, Moses Malone, and Doug Collins.

The Blazers won the first two games at home, but the 76ers responded by winning the next two at home.

However, the Blazers managed to win the last two games to win the series 4-2 and take home their first NBA championship.

Walton was named the Finals Most Valuable Player after averaging 18.5 points, 19.0 rebounds, and 5.2 assists per game in the series.

61

We find that the decade with the least wins was the 1950s with an average of 64.08% of victories, while the one that marks the milestone on the other side of the table is the 1980s with a 76.46% of wins.

The decade dominated by Magic Johnson and Larry Bird would only give us one champion with less than 70% of wins.

It was the 1982 Los Angeles Lakers, who signed a 57-25 (69.5%) in the regular season.

On the other side of the scale, and ignoring a first decade in which the NBA was in full birth process, it is equally striking how the 1970s are the only decade that drops below 70%, exactly 67.78%, since the one that started the League.

In those years, the curiosity arises that between 1975 and 1978 there were up to 3 champions that didn't even reach 60% of victories.

62

Since the Houston Rockets won in 1995 after finishing below 60% of wins, in their case a 57.3% with a record of 47-35, no other team has reached the top after such a weak regular season.

To find a similar case, but not equal, we have to go back to the 2005-06 season.

In that season, the Miami Heat had acquired Shaquille O'Neal, and between him and an excellent Dwyane Wade, they led the Florida team to the championship by defeating the Dallas Mavericks 4-2 in the Finals.

In those playoffs, which meant the first championship for the Heat, they were not favorites in the East.

Detroit signed a 64-18, San Antonio and Dallas also reached 60 victories, but none of that stopped them from becoming champions.

63

Denver Nuggets.

The Colorado-based franchise joined the competition in 1967 and has been in several situations where they could have had the number 1 draft pick, but it has always eluded them.

In the 1990-91 and 1997-98 seasons, they had the worst record in the NBA with a 20-62 and 11-71 record, respectively.

Having the highest percentage of options to choose from first place did not help them at all.

In 1991, they fell to the fourth spot to select Dikembe Mutombo, while in 1998, they went down to the third spot to acquire the services of Ralf Lafrentz.

It should be noted that none of the number 1 picks in those campaigns became big stars.

In '91, Larry Johnson, despite his great talent, was hindered by injuries, and in '98, Michael Olowakandi was nowhere near meeting expectations.

64

Indiana Pacers.

A historic organization that has never had
the first pick in a draft.

Also founded in 1967, the Indianapolis-based franchise
shares with Denver that, despite having had the worst
record in the competition twice, luck has eluded them.

After 17 years in the North American tournament,
the Pacers ended the 1983-84 season with
the worst record with 26-56.

In that draft, there were players like Hakeem
Olajuwon or Michael Jordan.

However, Indiana had previously traded what would
turn out to be the second pick to Portland,
who chose Sam Bowie.

Just one year later, in 1985, they had the worst record
again, tied with the Warriors at 22-60.

This time they kept their pick, but in a lottery that would
go down in history due to the rumors surrounding it.

65

Oklahoma City Thunder (Seattle Supersonics).

In 1967, the then-Seattle Supersonics, who were fighting to have an NBA team again, became one of the two franchises that have won a championship ring (1979) without having enjoyed a first pick.

Unlike the previous cases, this franchise has never finished with the worst record in a season, so they have never had the highest number of probabilities to be the first to choose.

Despite this, they have had fantastic players in their history, such as Gary Payton, number 2 in 1990 with whom they reached the 1996 Finals.

In 2007, they selected Kevin Durant also with the number 2 pick, and they also acquired Russell Westbrook and James Harden via draft.

In their new location, Oklahoma City, they repeated in the Finals in 2012.

66

Utah Jazz.

They are a professional basketball franchise
based in Salt Lake City, Utah.

They were founded in 1974 as the New Orleans
Jazz before moving to Utah in 1979.

The Jazz have won 9 division titles, 2 conference titles,
and have reached the NBA Finals twice, in 1997 and 1998,
losing both times to Michael Jordan's Chicago Bulls.

The history of the Jazz is marked by great players like John
Stockton and Karl Malone, who led the team
for much of the 1980s and 1990s.

They have also had other standout players like Pete
Maravich, Deron Williams, Carlos Boozer,
and Donovan Mitchell.

In recent years, the Jazz have been a competitive team in
the Western Conference of the NBA, led by coach Quin
Snyder and the backcourt duo of Donovan Mitchell
and Mike Conley.

In the 2020-2021 season, the Jazz finished with the best
record in the league at 52-20, but were eliminated in the
Western Conference semifinals by the Los Angeles Clippers.

67

Miami Heat.

Arriving in the NBA in 1988, the Florida-based team has also not been fortunate enough to be awarded the number 1 pick in the draft lottery.

The closest they came, by percentage of probability, was in 1989.

It was their first year in the competition and they finished with the worst record, signing a 15-67.

Destiny saw them fall to the fourth place, a position that, however, allowed them to acquire Glen Rice, who had 6 really good seasons with the Heat.

The number 1 pick of that draft, Pervis Ellison, could only play 475 games in his career due to injuries.

Miami has never picked first, but that has not prevented them from drafting the best player in their history.

In 2003, in one of the best drafts in history, the Florida team acquired Dwayne Wade with the 5th pick.

Flash led the Heat to their first championship and won 2 more after the arrival of LeBron James.

68

Memphis Grizzlies.

Landing in the NBA from the Canadian city of Vancouver, they have finished the regular season with the worst record on up to 4 occasions without luck smiling upon them in any of them.

In the first one, in 1996, they got Shareef Abdul Rahim with the 3rd pick while Philadelphia got Allen Iverson in the first pick.

A few years later, they signed a 14-68 record that only got them a number 4 pick that translated into Antonio Daniels.

In 1999, with the lockout in place, they said goodbye to the top spot and got Steve Francis with the 2nd pick.

It sounded good, but the point guard refused to play in Vancouver and the franchise traded him to Houston.

In 4 years, they said goodbye to Iverson, Duncan, and Francis.

69

Phoenix and New Orleans, recently debuted.

What are now 6 teams were until 2018 a list of 8.

That year, the Phoenix Suns, another team that until then had never been able to pick ahead of everyone else, used their worst record in the regular season (21-61) to select DeAndre Ayton with the 1st pick, a center who still has yet to prove himself but has shown promise so far.

In 2019, it was New Orleans Pelicans' turn to debut in the always difficult decision of choosing a player when everyone was available.

In their case, there were few doubts.

With Zion Williamson on the line, a guy destined to make a mark in the NBA and who is demonstrating it, the Louisiana team went for him.

He couldn't play too many games in his rookie year due to physical problems, but in the games he has played, he has simply amazed.

70

Ben Wallace is among the greatest players in history to achieve glory without being drafted.

In the case of Big Ben, we are talking about a guy who spent his college years at the modest Virginia Union of the NCAA Division II, where the reality is that he didn't make much noise.

With that small reputation, no franchise paid attention to his presence during the 1996 draft, which was helped by the fact that he was a 2.06 center (interior guys with more height were preferred).

Seeing that it was tough to make a spot in the NBA, he went to Europe for a few months, where he tried out with Reggio Calabria before finally being signed as a free agent by Washington.

There, during three seasons, he increased his role in the team until he left for Orlando in 1999, where he became an undisputed starter for the first time, averaging 4.8 points and 8.2 rebounds.

However, it would not be until the following season, in Detroit, when he would become one of the best defenders in the NBA.

71

John Starks.

The story of this boy from Tulsa, Oklahoma, begins with his college career where he played for up to 4 teams, something that certainly did not help his chances in the 1987 draft, in which he was not selected by any team.

With no place in the NBA, he opted to play in the CBA, a minor professional basketball league that existed from 1946 to 2010 and until 2000 served as a development league for the NBA.

After that momentary exit, he joined the Warriors in 1988, where he had barely any opportunities.

It was in the 1990-91 season when his career took a turn.

That year, he became part of the Knicks, where an injury sustained in a training session with Patrick Ewing prevented the team from releasing him.

By the time he recovered, his role had changed to replacing Gerald Wilkins, the team's starting shooting guard who had been injured.

That was the moment when he could display his talent and earn a spot on the team, eventually completing 8 seasons.

72

Brad Miller.

Trained at the reputable Purdue University, he shone there to the point of being the only player to have achieved at least 1,500 points, 800 rebounds, and 250 assists in the institution's history; a great achievement that, however, did not serve him to convince any team to choose him in the 1998 draft.

Despite not having that initial confidence, he still managed to secure a contract with Charlotte Hornets for that first year, where he would spend two seasons before playing for the same period of time in Chicago Bulls and Indiana Pacers.

In his second year, with the Indianapolis franchise, he became an All-Star for the first time, averaging 13.1 points, 8.3 rebounds, and 2.6 assists; a recognition that he would repeat the following season with the Sacramento Kings, achieving an average of 14.1 points, 10.3 rebounds, 4.3 assists, and 1.2 blocks.

.

73

Avery Johnson.

The point guard of those Spurs who won their first championship in 1999, was also not selected when he entered the 1988 draft.

Although in the two years he spent in college, he averaged 9.2 points, 12 assists, and 3.1 steals, his name did not ring a bell in 1988, but his career did not sink.

That same year, he signed with the Seattle Supersonics, where he barely had any minutes.

Denver, Houston, San Antonio (where he spent three stints), and Golden State had him in their ranks before he finally settled in the Spurs starting from 1994.

There, a period of 7 years opened up, culminating in the 1999 championship against the New York Knicks.

74

Bruce Bowen.

Without being selected in the 1993 draft, this Californian player spent 2 years playing in France and also tried his luck in the CBA before the Miami Heat gave him the opportunity to make his NBA debut in the 1996-97 season, albeit with only one minute in a single game.

The following year, in Boston, he played considerably more before also playing for Philadelphia and returning to Miami, where he began to make it clear what kind of player he was with a final season where he started in 72 games, averaging 32.7 minutes.

That breakout in the league helped him sign with the Spurs in 2001, where he would be a key player, starting in every game until the 2008-09 season, to win championships in 2003, 2005, and 2007.

75

Udonis Haslem had a great 4-year career in the NCAA, even being nominated for Naismith of the year, so it was expected that some team would trust in his abilities in the 2002 draft, but it didn't happen.

To reach the NBA, he had to spend 1 year in France with an impressive average of 16.1 points and 9.4 rebounds.

After showing his skills, the Miami Heat signed him in 2003, and they didn't regret it.

With his entire career in the Florida franchise, the last few years being mostly symbolic, he was very important in the 2006 championship, playing 29.5 minutes per night in that postseason to average 8.6 points and 7.4 rebounds.

Beyond his statistics, he routinely achieved double-doubles and his personality and leadership stood out, which he shared with Dwyane Wade during the Heat's best years in history.

76

John Wooden is widely considered one of the most successful and respected coaches in basketball history.

Born in 1910 in Indiana, Wooden had a career as a college basketball player before becoming a coach in 1946.

After coaching at various high schools and colleges, Wooden became the coach at the University of California, Los Angeles (UCLA) in 1948.

There, he achieved one of the most impressive records in sports history, guiding the Bruins to 10 consecutive national championships between 1964 and 1975.

Wooden's coaching philosophy emphasized the importance of teamwork, discipline, and work ethic.

He also emphasized the importance of technique and mastery of the basic fundamentals of basketball.

Wooden was known for his focus on the personal development of his players and was a master of motivation and leadership.

Wooden was inducted into the Basketball Hall of Fame in 1960 as a player and in 1973 as a coach.

After retiring from coaching, Wooden became a popular author and speaker, and his books and talks are considered a source of inspiration for many basketball coaches and players.

Wooden passed away in 2010 at the age of 99.

77

David Wesley had to go through the CBA and the Venezuelan league before the Nets gave him the opportunity to debut in the NBA in 1993, although with little participation.

It would be with the Boston Celtics, where he spent the next 3 years, that he would explode as a great scorer capable of also playing as a playmaker; in the 1996–97 season, he averaged 16.8 points, 7.3 assists, 3.6 rebounds, and 2.2 steals.

Already established as one of the important players in the league, he would spend the best years of his career with the Charlotte Hornets, where he played for 8 seasons.

There, alongside Baron Davis and Jamal Mashburn, he would reach the Eastern Conference semifinals on 2 occasions.

Especially painful was the defeat in 2001 against the Milwaukee Bucks, losing 4–3.

He would finish his career playing 1 year in Houston and another in Cleveland, a team he was a part of in the year they reached their first Finals with LeBron James, although Wesley did not participate in that postseason.

78

Raja Bell.

His opportunity in the NBA came from the Philadelphia 76ers,
where he spent two seasons with little playing time,
just like the following season with the Dallas Mavericks.

The turning point in his career came with
his arrival in Salt Lake City.

In the 2003-04 season, his first with the Jazz, he left the shadow
of Texas to sign 11.2 points, 2.9 rebounds, and 1.3 assists
in 24.2 minutes per night.

It was the beginning of a series of seasons in which
he established himself in the league as a starter.

Success and recognition would come in Phoenix.

With the Suns, he spent four seasons playing in the
Western Conference Finals in 2006, falling 4-2 to Dallas.

A year later, in 2007, he was included in the All-Defensive
Team of the season.

He would end his journey through the competition in 2012,
once again as a member of the Jazz.

79

José Manuel Calderón.

The Spanish point guard entered the draft in 2003 without being selected.

By then, he was already an established player in the ACB league and would play two more seasons of his five total before making the leap to the NBA, which would take place in 2005.

It was the Toronto Raptors who noticed him and in August of that year closed his contract.

There, in Canada, he found a home.

He spent up to 7 and a half seasons with the Raptors, in which he would play in the playoffs twice without getting past the first round.

He left the Canadian franchise in the middle of the 2012–13 season with an average of 10 points and 7.2 assists, the latter being second in the franchise's history with 3,770 assists.

After leaving Toronto, he went through Detroit, Dallas, New York, Los Angeles, Atlanta, Cleveland, and again Detroit before announcing his retirement in November 2019.

80

Darrell Armstrong.

From being forgotten by everyone to being one
of the emblems of the Orlando Magic
for several years.

That is the case of Darrell Armstrong, a guy who
did not play basketball until his last year of high
school, who was forgotten in the 1993 draft and
who did not start to stand out in the NBA until
1997 when he arrived with the Florida franchise
in the 1994-95 season where he would
only play three games.

Despite that erratic start and being forced to
migrate to Europe, playing in Ourense,
Armstrong knew how to make a place for
himself in the NBA, slowly carving out a spot;
so much so that in the 1998-99 season, he was
named both Sixth Man of the Year and Most
Improved Player, a combination of awards that
no one else has achieved in NBA history.

81

Wesley Matthews is an American professional basketball player currently playing for the Los Angeles Lakers of the NBA.

Born on October 14, 1986 in San Antonio, Texas, Matthews attended Marquette University where he played for the Golden Eagles basketball team.

After going undrafted in the 2009 NBA draft, Matthews signed as a free agent with the Utah Jazz where he had a good rookie season.

However, in 2010, the Portland Trail Blazers offered Matthews a four-year, $34 million contract which the Jazz did not match.

Matthews played for the Blazers for five seasons, where he established himself as one of the league's best three-point shooters.

In 2015, Matthews signed with the Dallas Mavericks and spent three seasons there before being waived in 2018.

He then spent a season with the Indiana Pacers before signing with the Milwaukee Bucks for the 2019-2020 season.

After a year with the Bucks, Matthews signed a contract with the Lakers in December 2020.

Throughout his career, Matthews has been recognized for his defensive ability and his ability to score from long distance.

He has also participated in several three-point contests at the NBA All-Star Weekend.

82

**Kent Bazemore's career would change
drastically in February 2014.**

The Lakers, a team that year with virtually no chance
of making the playoffs, traded for him and played
him for 28 minutes per game.

What was the result for the North Carolina kid?

He averaged 13.1 points, 3.3 rebounds, 3.1 assists,
and 1.3 steals.

That great end to the season served him well
as the Atlanta Hawks took notice.

There in Georgia, he spent five seasons present in the
60-win campaign, which would conclude in the Eastern
Conference Finals, as well as in
two other postseason runs.

In his last four years with the Hawks, he averaged
over 11 points, establishing himself as a starter.

He has also played with the Sacramento Kings,
where he contributes 10.3 points and 5 rebounds
off the bench.

83

**Fred VanVleet, the Toronto player,
is from Illinois.**

In 2016, the Raptors called him up for the
Las Vegas Summer League, and in
November of that same year, he made
his debut against the Thunder.

In that first season, he only played 37
games, a meager participation that would
change drastically in the following season,
especially in the 2018-19 season.

VanVleet was instrumental in
Toronto's championship title.

After several poor performances, he
signed a 53% three-point percentage in
the last 9 games, and in the sixth game
against Golden State, he scored 22 points.

84

Kendrick Nunn is a professional basketball player who currently plays as a point guard for the Miami Heat in the NBA.

He was born on August 3, 1995 in Chicago, Illinois, and attended Oakland University where he played college basketball.

After going undrafted in the 2018 NBA draft, Nunn joined the Santa Cruz Warriors of the G League.

There, he averaged 19.3 points, 3.8 rebounds, and 2.8 assists per game, which caught the attention of NBA teams.

In the 2019-2020 season, Nunn signed with the Miami Heat and quickly became one of the league's top rookies.

He started in 62 of the 67 games he played, averaging 15.3 points, 3.3 rebounds, and 2.7 assists per game, which earned him a spot on the NBA All-Rookie second team.

In the 2020-2021 season, Nunn lost his starting position with the arrival of star player Victor Oladipo and injuries, but still averaged 14.6 points, 3.2 rebounds, and 2.6 assists per game.

He is currently an important piece in the Miami Heat rotation as the sixth man and continues to demonstrate his scoring ability and skill in creating plays for his teammates.

85

Jerry West, born in West Virginia in 1938, played 14 seasons in the league with the Los Angeles Lakers and is considered one of the greatest players in history and undoubtedly one of the greatest scorers of all time.

He finished his career with an average of 27 points per game (4 seasons above 30) and is still the leading scorer in the Finals with 1,679 points.

However, all of his impressive qualities only led him to be champion once.

86

Elgin Baylor arrived at the Lakers in 1958, when they were still in Minneapolis, and he quickly became a star.

In his first year, he was the fourth highest scorer in the league (24.9 points), the third in rebounds (15), and the eighth in assists (4.1).

Of course, he was named Rookie of the Year and began a path of dominance on the court that, however, was not enough to win a championship.

Although he never won a Finals, Baylor held the honorary title of being the player who scored the most points in a Finals game.

87

LeBron James has reached 8 consecutive Finals out of the 9 he has played, but fate has wanted him to come up short of the ring 6 times.

The first time was when James had only been in the league for 4 years, and he lost 4-0 to the San Antonio Spurs.

Then, from 2011 to 2018, he played 4 with the Miami Heat (winning 2 and losing 2) and 4 more with the Cleveland Cavaliers (winning 1 and losing 3).

In the last era with the Cavs, in all the Finals the Golden State Warriors were the favorites, and even more so after acquiring the services of Kevin Durant in 2016.

88

Larry Foust.

In 1950, the Fort Wayne Pistons acquired Larry Foust, a 2.05-meter center who immediately became one of the best interior players in the league.

In the state of Indiana, where he spent 7 years, he would play in 2 Finals.

In the first one (1956), they lost 4-3 against the Syracuse Nationals, and in the second one (1957), they lost 4-1 against the Philadelphia Warriors.

In 1959, while playing for the Lakers, he lost 4-0 against the Boston Celtics.

It would be the Celtics who would deny him a championship ring again in 1960 and 1961, when he had joined the San Louis Hawks.

Five Finals with three different teams and 0 victories.

89

Pau Gasol.

He is a retired Spanish basketball player, born in Barcelona in 1980.

He is one of the most successful and recognized players in the history
of Spanish and European basketball, and one of the
most prominent in the NBA.

Gasol began his basketball career in Spain, playing for FC Barcelona and
winning two ACB League championships before being selected
third overall in the 2001 NBA draft by the Memphis Grizzlies.

In Memphis, he quickly became one of the team's stars and one of the
best players in the NBA, averaging more than 20 points
and 10 rebounds per game for several seasons.

In 2008, Gasol was traded to the Los Angeles Lakers, where he joined
Kobe Bryant to form one of the most lethal duos in the NBA.

With the Lakers, he won two consecutive championships in 2009 and
2010, and was selected to the All-Star Game three times.

In total, Gasol played 18 seasons in the NBA with the Grizzlies, Lakers,
Chicago Bulls, San Antonio Spurs, and Milwaukee Bucks.

In addition to his success in the NBA, Gasol has been a cornerstone of
the Spanish national basketball team, winning two silver medals in the
2008 and 2012 Olympics, as well as a world championship in 2006
and three European championships in 2009, 2011, and 2015.

He has also been awarded numerous awards and recognitions throughout
his career, including twice being named the European Player of the Year
and the Gold Medal of the Royal Order of Sporting Merit in Spain.

In 2019, he announced his retirement from professional basketball.

90

Magic Johnson.

The showtime arrived with him, but beyond the spectacle he offered every time he stepped onto the court, he was a born competitor.

In 13 playoff runs, he was able to reach the Finals in nine of them.

He emerged victorious in 5 of them and lost 4, with his legendary matchups with Larry Bird's Celtics being particularly memorable.

They faced each other in the Finals 3 times in a 4-year period.

Ending his career with an average of 19.5 points, 11.2 assists, 7.2 rebounds, and 1.2 steals, Magic accumulated 12 All-Star selections, was MVP of the game in 2 of them, won 3 regular season MVPs and 3 Finals MVPs.

Undoubtedly, one of the greatest in the game.

91

Kareem Abdul-Jabbar.

In his 20-year NBA career, Kareem
Abdul-Jabbar had time to coincide with
the last years of Wilt Chamberlain in the
NBA as part of the Milwaukee Bucks,
lead a transitional Lakers team just after
Chamberlain's retirement, and live
the best years of showtime
alongside Magic Johnson.

In that extensive period of time, he
reached the Finals up to 10 times,
winning 6 rings (one with the Bucks
and 5 with the Lakers) and seeing
how he fell short on 4 occasions.

92

Danny Ainge.

Arriving in the NBA in 1981, he was a key member of Larry Bird's Celtics, with whom he won 2 rings and lost 2 other Finals, both against the Los Angeles Lakers in 1985 and 1987.

Despite his more than relevant participation with Boston, he was traded to the Sacramento Kings in 1989.

After passing through California, he arrived in Portland in 1990 to play in the 1992 Finals, falling to Michael Jordan's Bulls.

And a few years later, as part of the Phoenix Suns, he lost again to the Illinois team 4-2.

93

Willis Reed.

A player who in the 1969-70 season achieved something that has only been seen again in the NBA with Michael Jordan (2 occasions) and Shaquille O'Neal, as he won the All-Star MVP, regular season MVP, and Finals MVP in the same year, thus giving New Yorkers their first title in history.

He won the first of those awards on January 20, 1970, at The Spectrum in Philadelphia, leading the Eastern Conference to victory by 142-135 by scoring 21 points and grabbing 11 rebounds in 30 minutes.

At that time, he shared the court with a cast of stars including Elgin Baylor, Jerry West, Oscar Robertson, and John Havlicek.

94

Chamberlain.

Arriving in the league in 1959, he set a milestone by being the regular season MVP in his debut season.

The truth is that the numbers he had accumulated didn't leave many other options.

Playing for the Philadelphia Warriors, he averaged 37.6 points and 27 rebounds for a record of 49-26, winning the vote over Bill Russell by 270 points to 186.

Without a doubt, it was the starting point of an enormous career that, however, was marked by the dominance of the Celtics, who would win up to 9 rings in the 60s.

95

Magic and Bird, the duel of the 80s.

As if it were the best-scripted movie, they competed against each other in college until they met in the Finals, they arrived in the NBA in the same year (1979), and they did it in the 2 most successful franchises in history: the Los Angeles Lakers and the Boston Celtics.

Their journey in the league ridiculed expectations.

Fierce competitors, though with opposite personalities, they turned the 80s into a legend, one in which each one contributed not a grain, but mountains of sand, for the popularity of the NBA and the public's interest in it to skyrocket.

Magic and Bird are on that shortlist of players who have managed to win all three MVP awards in the league.

96

Jordan's dominance.

We can enjoy and get to know it in a special way through the documentary The Last Dance, which focuses on the 1997-98 season.

However, his dominance and legend in the league began to be written much earlier; so much so that by 1991 he had already won 3 MVP trophies.

1988 was the year when his display of talent began to be recognized.

With Chicago as a witness, Michael stood out in the All-Star Game to win the MVP with nothing less than 40 points.

It was just the prelude to a season in which he led the Bulls to a record of 50-32, averaging the outrageous numbers of 35 points, 5.5 rebounds, 5.9 assists, and 3.2 steals to win the MVP, surpassing Bird (second) and Magic (third).

97

Shaquille, a beast on all terrains.

He brought a different touch to the NBA, one in which his physical power translated into something indefensible for his opponents.

Just after Michael's retirement, Shaq became a legend for the Lakers, leading them to the 2000, 2001, and 2002 championships, being the Finals MVP in all those occasions.

Those were his best seasons; so much so that in the 1999-2000 season, just before winning the championship, he won his only regular season MVP award by averaging 29.7 points (his career high), 13.6 rebounds, 3.8 assists (his career high), and 3 blocks.

With that exceptional performance, he led the Lakers to a record of 67-15, marking the beginning of what would become a three-peat.

But O'Neal was more than a fantastic player, he was pure entertainment.

With his friendly and joking personality, when the All-Star Game came, he was the first to give his all so that the fans could enjoy both on and off the court.

98

Tim Duncan.

By 1999, he had already won the first of his five rings.

By 2002, Duncan had already earned the 3 MVP awards.

The first award that came to his hands was
the Finals MVP.

Playing against the New York Knicks in 1999, this guy
from the Virgin Islands went up to 27.4 points,
14 rebounds, 2.4 assists, and 2.2 blocks to be
chosen as the best player of the series.

The following year, with Oakland as a witness, he would
also win the All-Star MVP, a honor that he would share
with another boss in the paint: Shaquille O'Neal.

And he had to wait little to complete his journey, as in
2002 he was named MVP of the regular season, signing
an average of 25.5 points, 12.7 rebounds, 3.9 assists, and
2.9 blocks, and leading San Antonio to a record of 58-24.

99

**Kobe, All-Star King Unfortunately,
died in a tragic helicopter accident.**

Kobe Bryant, Lakers legend, where he spent his entire
career, also managed to win all 3 MVP awards
distributed by the NBA.

While in his early years with the franchise he achieved
3 championship rings alongside Shaquille O'Neal, it was
not until he was without him on the team that his
figure grew to unimaginable limits.

To start his trophy collection, The Black Mamba would
win the All-Star Game's best player award in 2002.

At that time he was only 23 years old, which did not
prevent him from being the MVP of a game that
featured figures such as Kevin Garnett,
Allen Iverson, or Paul Pierce.

After that success for his resume, he had to wait for
five years to add to his collection of individual awards.

He would repeat in the All-Star Game on up to 3
occasions in the years 2007, 2009, and 2011, becoming
the player who has won it the most times
with 4 along with Bob Pettit.

100

LeBron.

He achieved the triple crown in 2012. A very special year for him as it marked his first championship.

In that campaign, in which he won his third regular season MVP, he would reach the Finals to face the Oklahoma City Thunder of Kevin Durant and Russell Westbrook, whom he defeated 4-1 averaging 28.6 points, 10.2 rebounds, and 7.4 assists to be chosen as the best player of the final series.

From there, he repeated as MVP of the season and the Finals in 2013.

As for the All-Star Game, he was selected as the best player of the game in 2006, 2008, and 2018.

101

The season in which the Spurs did not make the playoffs was the 1996-1997 season, when they finished with a record of 20 wins and 62 losses, which was the worst record in the NBA that year.

Since then, the Spurs have been one of the most successful teams in the league, winning five NBA championships in six finals played between 1999 and 2014.

Gregg Popovich has been the coach of the Spurs since the 1996-1997 season, and has been one of the most successful coaches in NBA history, with a record of 1370 wins and 635 losses until the end of the 2020-2021 season.

Tim Duncan, Tony Parker, and Manu Ginobili were the team leaders for many years, and all three players were members of the team during the five championships won.

If you have enjoyed the curiosities about the NBA presented in this book, we would like to ask you to share a review on Amazon.

Your opinion is very valuable to us and to other NBA enthusiasts who are looking to be entertained and learn new knowledge about this sport.

We understand that leaving a comment can be a tedious process, but we ask you to take a few minutes of your time to share your thoughts and opinions with us.

Your support is very important to us and helps us continue to create quality content for fans of this incredible sport.

We appreciate your support and hope you have enjoyed reading our book as much as we enjoyed writing it.

Thank you for sharing your experience with us!

Printed in Great Britain
by Amazon